DAVID THORPE
THE DEFEATED
LIFE RESTORED

PLATES

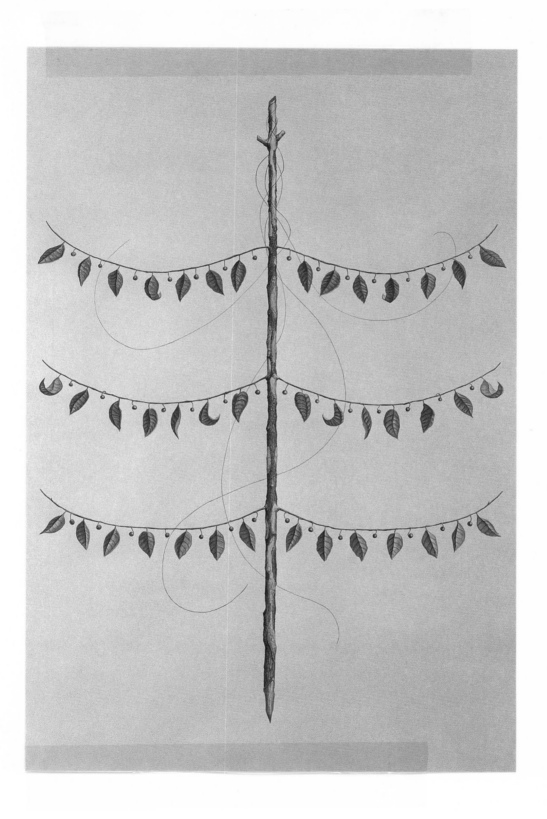

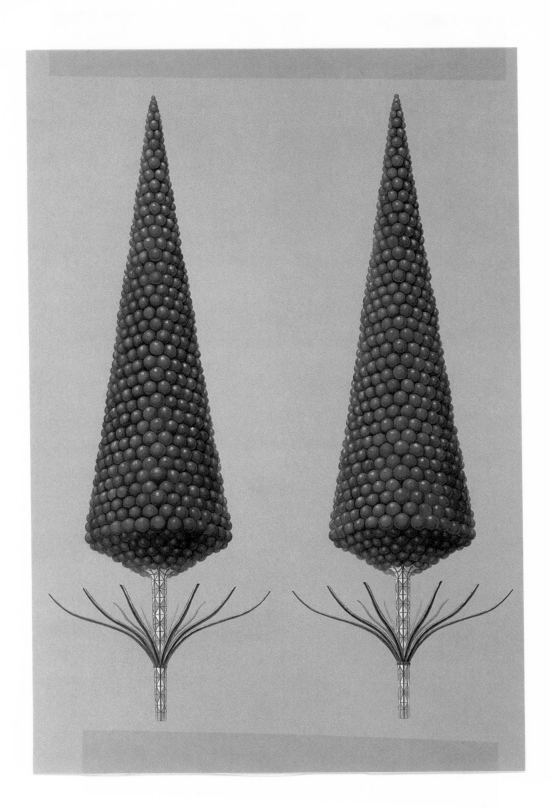

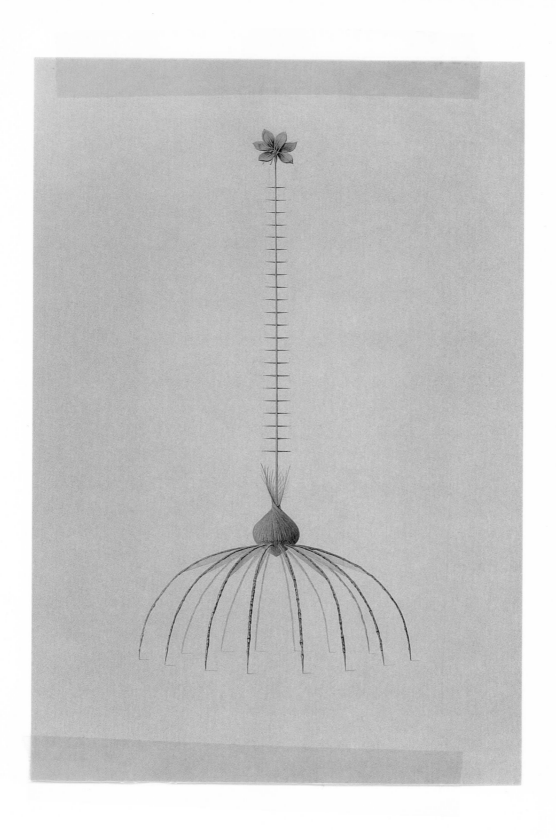

THE DEFEATED
LIFE RESTORED

CULTIVATION
CATHERINE WOOD
KULTIVIERUNG

CULTIVATION An 'allegorical impulse' is clearly manifest in the
CATHERINE WOOD work of David Thorpe. In fact, it would be truer
to say that allegory forms its structural basis. Woven through Thorpe's
collages, sculptures, drawings, poetry, architectural models and screens is
an implied narrative that conjures the notion of a 'world' of the artist's
making. Thorpe has written that for him "art has always been about
building up a protective universe to inhabit",[1] and has often spoken of
his practice, and his references, in terms that evoke an extended,
metaphorical fiction. This fiction is not the content, but the *enabler* of the
work's cultivation however, permitting Thorpe a reclusive engagement
with the practice of inventing and crafting objects and pictures.[2]

In *The Allegorical Impulse: Towards a Theory of Postmodernism* (1980),[3] Craig
Owens identified a key shift in art practice, from American high
modernist painterly abstraction to a new kind of mass-media derived
figuration, using montage techniques. Owens observed that allegory had
been a persistent feature of art history since medieval times, but had
latterly been suppressed by modernism's logic of form versus content.
"Allegory is extravagant, an expenditure of surplus value; it is always in
excess", he wrote.[4] Looking at artists such as Cindy Sherman, Robert
Longo and Sherrie Levine, Owens's analysis was fundamentally to do
with the way in which they re-ordered existing visual codes to deconstruct
familiar signs and symbols that shaped social relations and identity.
Owens distinguishes postmodernism from modernism via its references
to 'found' or observed culture, rather than being autonomously self-
referential and "self-critical".[5]

Thorpe's practice borrows from both categories in Owens's analysis: using
post-modern montage to weave together found references whilst pushing
the notion of modernism's 'autonomy' to a threatening extreme. But he
describes his engagement with like-minded people in quasi-religious
terms, as "a confederacy of seekers", and looks well beyond contemporary
culture in his multiple points of cross-historical and cross-cultural identification. References range from 17th-century political pamphlets and
botanical drawings to religious paintings or science fiction, described as
his "friends of liberty".[6] The artist has also written about making art
in terms of a "military defence strategy".[7] At the same time, Thorpe's
position in the studio is wilfully isolationist – his own work and the work
of others serving as "lifelines of communication and sustenance".[8] The
allegorical nature of this practice is not to be found as a simple,
detachable 'surplus' that tells a readable story. Rather, Thorpe's use of
allegory is fundamental: the very creation of the medium is permitted by
the underlying message.

Among Thorpe's "friends of liberty", he lists the American Quaker
artist Edward Hicks (1780-1849). Hicks is known for his painted series
titled *The Peaceable Kingdom* that illustrates a passage from Isaiah (11:6) – an
image he returned to repeatedly throughout his life, painting it over one
hundred times. This picture, bordered with an explanatory text, tells of
a prophecy in which wild and tame animals sit peacefully together:

"The wolf also shall dwell with the lamb / And the leopard shall lie down with the kid / And the calf and the young lion and the fatling together".

For Hicks, the return to this scene was an attempt to synthesize the technically limited means of his art with his all consuming religious belief. Like the curious creatures in Henri Rousseau's jungle paintings that were invented with reference only to illustrations in journals and visits to the Paris Zoo, it is the resulting awkward tension between vision and execution that makes Hicks's world so compelling. That Hicks started life as a sign painter makes sense of his repeated refining of the image to its essentials. This is akin to a development of an iconic 'logo' that stands for the work's allegorical content and marries with Craig Owens's identification of the vertical layering of significance at play in allegorical figuration: the collage of image and narrative into "a single emblematic instant" which Roland Barthes, he notes, calls a "hieroglyph".[9]

It is in terms of a shared persistence of vision that the development of Thorpe's work in the past ten years might be seen to parallel Hicks's project. Rather than developing 'logically' into either simpler abstractions or more intricately representational images, the earliest collages of the 1990s have grown into environmental installations that have made the emblematic form of the artist's world manifest in three dimensions, evolving significantly from their original basis in observational drawing. In cutting and pasting coloured sugar paper to make his own cityscapes, sometimes resembling simplified film stills, Thorpe discovered a method of claiming the promise that widely-consumed media images offered: of building a tangible link between their imaginary world and his existence in real time. These painstakingly cut and pasted pictures represented fantastical projections of the architectural skyline of South East London where he lived, blending local and mass-cultural references. In forging such links between imagined and 'found' imagery, Thorpe began his longer term exploration of the meeting point between the individual agency and the world as a given entity.

His collages from the mid-late 1990s depict large-scale structures which propose the possibility of enjoyment – some by creative ingenuity on the part of the participants, some by design. Silhouetted nightscapes of people at funfairs and in cable cars appeared alongside compositions of practical architectural structures re-claimed by city inhabitants so as to propose a form of *detournément* in the urban environment: pylons imagined as gigantic climbing frames in *Fun*, or a motorway flyover as a viewing spot for a shooting star in *Need for Speed*. Later, Thorpe's engagement with his materials began to take on greater complexity, moving towards the intense layering evident in his pictures made between 2004-06. Image sources shifted from the city towards grand wildernesses with curious architectural structures set within them. In *Out from the Night the Day is Beautiful ...* (1999), showing a hang-glider set against soaring pines in a mountain landscape, the complex arrangement of tiny pieces creates a contoured surface with a resemblance to camouflage.

In their increasingly intricate construction, involving a variety of new materials, the thickening surface of the collages might be seen to have led Thorpe's practice to turn – productively – in on itself. If his project began by reaching towards an unobtainable image-world – the 'spectacle' of mass culture represented in shared popular culture – the development from this point might be that the artist began to understand the extent to which the manipulation of materials could offer endless possibilities of invention in itself. Collages made between 2004-06 incorporate tissue paper, dried bark, mass-produced jewellery, slate, glass and dried grasses or flowers. Thorpe's increasingly dense installations, such as *The Colonist* (2004) or *The Defeated Life Restored* (2007) demonstrate the extent to which the artist's world has expanded from one that can be represented as a two-dimensional image towards one that inhabits the gallery space in 'four' dimensions, manifested in a combination of pictures, sculptures, screens and hand-painted posters bearing declarative poetic text.

The introduction and consolidation of integral architectural elements in the form of wood and glass screens that mark out and intersect a space in which the drawing, sculpture and collage are shown, indicates the extent to which the 'world' of Thorpe's work now appears to be self-sufficient. In opposition to the contemporary tradition of responsive site-specificity, the heraldic nature of Thorpe's installation design imposes itself on the space in which it is exhibited, rejecting its physical qualities as givens. The more-or-less symmetrical layout of *The Defeated Life Restored* presents this in its most extreme manifestation to date; pulling the viewer's experience inside the work away from its awareness of the existing architectural elements such as the placement of doors or windows, and obscuring conventional white surfaces with substituted screen-walls that insist upon a demarcated space matching the work's own shape, texture and pattern. The three mosaic patterned 'missile' sculptures placed within the screens have the solidity and permanence of architectural columns.

Within his installations, the objects and pictures set up complex chains of connection that exaggerate the underlying fiction of self-sufficiency with more literal survivalist implications. Allegorical surplus folds itself back through each conception. The sculptures double as practical objects which might feature in the world of his landscape images, and as simple aesthetic objects. Continuous shifts in scale – from a house pictured in a collage, to an abstract architectural model, to a large-scale screen – frustrate the possibility of concrete moments of representational realism that might be tied to an existing reference. Thorpe's earlier watercolours appeared to offer some truth as 'pure' specimens of the natural biology of the world from his vision. But studied closely, these plants are grown from, and shot through with, the geometries of man-made culture. In recent watercolours the plants have begun to take more elaborately designed forms that present them as a set of insignia, as though they are coded with the genetic structure that forms a basis of potential applicability for all the artist's imaginatively generated schemes or plans and, at the same time, bear witness to some familial heritage.

~

The opacity created by Thorpe's defensive, ornamental fortification might be understood on one level as a counterpoint to its material fragility. It manifests the artist's awareness of the precious vulnerability of this nature of creation as an island of specialist activity within the real economy of labour and exchange. As is evident in the painstaking detail on the surfaces of his objects, the sense of joy in craft tips over into almost a counter-productive obsession and points to Thorpe's acknowledgement of the artist-labourer's position as a luxurious and therefore necessarily protected and slightly paranoid one. Thorpe's attitude to 'work' opens up a different kind of time than that which is measured, and speeded on, by the mechanised regularity of late capitalism. Interrupting the pace of production and the spectacle of consumerism, the images and objects he makes are slow and hard to digest. The secretive nature of the work's multiple locked references, reaching back into history and laterally towards diverse pockets of subculture to find material points of identification, go against the grain of contemporary notions of 'participatory' practice with democratic appeal. Instead, the work extends a double-edged invitation and warding-off of communality – akin to Sun Ra's conception of his own philosophy offering "a bridge to some, a wall to others".

In *The Mighty Lights Community Project* (2003) the artist staged, as a performance, an imaginary 'meeting' of the inhabitants of his world.[10] Participants wearing matching t-shirts star-jumped in formation as they sang hymns and chants, typical of Thorpe's own poems, on the ambiguously enthusiastic and sinister theme of utopian communal living and belief in a shared, glorious future. The allegorical impulse in Thorpe's work allows such a fantasy of community to 'explain' the work's existence in the kind of human terms that recent art discourse does not permit. Underwritten by fiction, the work can be more romantic, more mysterious, more beautiful, more un-place-able or unreadable that it could otherwise rationally be. Like Thorpe's plant specimens that 'grow' designs for houses, his fiction enables his art to flourish. Quite distinct from the early modernist project of the Russian constructivists, for example, who envisioned a new world that would be jolted into recognition by their revolutionary abstract designs applied to everything from political posters to workers clothing to interior design, Thorpe creates an art that exists – in parentheses – as the simultaneous *product* of his ideal community and the blueprint for its *potential*: not proposing a radical or critically deconstructive break with the past but dragging out and framing a new set of aesthetic relationships and positions from within it.

[1] Interview with Rainald Schumacher, exh. cat. "Imagination Becomes Reality: Part III", Munich (Sammlung Goetz) 2006, p. 183. [2] I note in my *Frieze* review of The Colonists, Thorpe's Meyer Riegger, Karlsruhe show of 2004, that he uses the idea of 'cultivation' as though it has a corrupted etymology, "combining cult and culture". Catherine Wood, *David Thorpe: Meyer Riegger, Karlsruhe, Frieze,* No. 84, June – August, 2004. [3] Parts 1 and 2 were published in *October*, issues 12 and 13 (Spring/ Summer 1980). [4] ibid. p. 64. [5] ibid p. 85. [6] Goetz cat ref, interview with Rainald Schumacher, p. 183. [7] David Thorpe, *The Kingdom of Seekers, Metropolis M,* No. 2 April/May, 2004. [8] As I described in my text for Thorpe's exhibition in Art Now space, Tate Gallery, London. [9] Craig Owens, "Beyond Recognition: Representation, Power, and Culture", 1994, p. 58. [10] Tate Britain, as a part of Tate & Egg Live, 2003.

KULTIVIERUNG Im Werk von David Thorpe ist deutlich ein
CATHERINE WOOD »allegorischer Impuls« zu erkennen. Genauer
gesagt, bildet die Allegorie dessen strukturelle Grundlage. Thorpes
Collagen, Skulpturen, Zeichnungen, Gedichte, Architekturmodelle und
Wandschirme sind durchwebt von einer impliziten Erzählung, die den
Gedanken an eine vom Künstler geschaffene »Welt« nahe legt. »Für mich
ging es beim Erschaffen von Kunst immer darum, eine Schutzzone
herzustellen, ein bewohnbares Universum«[1], schrieb Thorpe, und er sprach
von seiner Praxis und seinen Bezugspunkten oft in Worten, die an eine
ausgedehnte metaphorische Fiktion denken lassen. Diese Fiktion ist nicht
der Inhalt, sondern die *Möglichkeitsbedingung* der Kultivierung des Werks[2];
kraft ihrer kann Thorpe sich in einem einsiedlerischen Engagement der
Erfindung und Anfertigung von Objekten und Bildern widmen.

In *The Allegorical Impulse: Towards a Theory of Postmodernism*[3] stellte Craig
Owens 1980 fest, dass in der Welt der Kunst eine grundlegende Ver-
schiebung stattfand, nämlich von der malerischen Abstraktion auf dem
Höhepunkt des amerikanischen Modernismus zu einer aus den Massen-
medien abgeleiteten Figuration neuer Art, die mit Collagetechniken
arbeitet. Owens beobachtete, dass die Allegorie seit dem Mittelalter ein
ständiges Merkmal der Kunstgeschichte bildet, später aber durch die
Form-versus-Inhalt-Logik der Moderne unterbunden wurde. »Allegorie
ist extravagant, eine Vergabe von Mehrwert; sie ist stets überschüssig«,
schrieb er[4]. Mit Blick auf Künstler wie Cindy Sherman, Robert Longo
oder Sherrie Levine beleuchtete Owens' Analyse gründlich, auf welche
Weise diese bestehende visuelle Codes neu ordneten, um vertraute
Zeichen und Symbole, die soziale Beziehungen und Identität formten,
zu dekonstruieren. Owens unterscheidet die Postmoderne insofern von
der Moderne, als erstere sich auf eine »(vor-) gefundene« oder
beobachtete Kultur bezieht, anstatt eine selbstreferentielle und »selbst-
kritische«[5] Autonomie geltend zu machen.

Thorpes Praxis belehnt beide Kategorien, wie Owen sie analysiert: Er
benutzt die postmoderne Montage, um (vor-) gefundene Referenzen
miteinander zu verweben, und treibt gleichwohl den »Autonomie«-
Gedanken der Moderne zu einem bedrohlichen Extrem voran. Dabei
beschreibt er seinen Umgang mit Gleichgesinnten in quasi-religiösen
Begriffen als »Bündnis von Suchern« und blickt in seinen zahlreichen,
quer durch Geschichte und Kultur verteilten Identifikationspunkten
weit über die zeitgenössische Kultur hinaus. Die Quellen reichen von
politischen Streitschriften und botanischen Zeichnungen aus dem 17.
Jahrhundert bis zu religiösen Gemälden oder Science Fiction – seine
»Freunde der Freiheit«[6], wie er sie nennt. Auch über die Ausübung von
Kunst als »militärische Abwehrstrategie«[7] hat der Künstler geschrieben.
Gleichzeitig bezieht Thorpe im Atelier eine gewollt isolationistische
Stellung, wobei sein Werk und das von anderen als »Lebenslinien der
Kommunikation und Ernährung«[8] dienen. Die allegorische Beschaf-
fenheit dieser Praxis kommt nicht als ablösbare »Dreingabe« daher,
die eine fertig lesbare Geschichte erzählt. Vielmehr benutzt Thorpe die

Allegorie als Fundament: Die Herausbildung des Mediums selbst wird durch die zugrunde liegende Botschaft gewährt.

~

Unter seinen »Freunden der Freiheit« nennt Thorpe auch den amerikanischen Quäkerkünstler Edward Hicks (1780-1849). Hicks ist bekannt für seine Gemäldeserie *The Peacable Kingdom*, die eine Stelle im Buch Jesaja (11,6) illustriert – ein Bild, das er im Lauf seines Lebens immer wieder aufgriff und ingesamt über hundert Mal malte. Von einem erläuternden Text gesäumt, schildert es eine Prophezeiung, in der wilde und zahme Tiere friedlich miteinander siedeln:

Da werden die Wölfe bei den Lämmern wohnen und die Panther bei den Böcken lagern. Ein kleiner Knabe wird Kälber und junge Löwen und Mastvieh miteinander treiben.

Für Hicks war die Rückbesinnung auf diese Szene ein Versuch, die technisch beschränkten Mittel seiner Kunst mit seinem alles verzehrenden religiösen Glauben in Einklang zu bringen. Wie bei den merkwürdigen Geschöpfen in Henri Rousseaus Dschungelbildern, die nur aus Illustrationen in Zeitschriften und anhand von Besuchen im Pariser Zoo entwickelt wurden, ist es die befremdende Spannung zwischen Anschauung und Ausführung, die Hicks' Werk so zwingend macht. Hicks begann sein Berufsleben als Schildermaler, und so leuchtet ein, weshalb er seine Bilder immer wieder auf ihre Wesensmerkmale verschlankte. Er erarbeitete gewissermaßen ein für den allegorischen Inhalt des Werks stehendes ikonisches »Logo«. Dieses Verfahren verschränkt sich mit Craig Owens' Definition der vertikalen Bedeutungsschichtung, die in der allegorischen Darstellung zum Zuge kommt: die Collage – Verklebung – von Bild und Erzählung zu einem »einzigen emblematischen Moment«, den Roland Barthes, wie er vermerkt, als »Hieroglyphe« bezeichnet[9].

Es ist eine vergleichbare Nachhaltigkeit der Anschauung, die den Gedanken nahelegt, dass Thorpes Werk in den letzten zehn Jahren möglicherweise einen parallelen Weg zu Hicks' Projekt eingeschlagen hat. Anstatt sich »folgerichtig« zu einfacheren Abstraktionen oder vertrackteren gegenständlichen Bildern zu entwickeln, haben sich die frühesten Collagen, entstanden in den neunziger Jahren, zu raumgreifenden Installationen ausgewachsen, die die emblematische Form der Welt des Künstlers in drei Dimensionen manifestieren und dabei doch unverkennbar aus ihrer ursprünglichen Grundlage im beobachtenden Zeichnen hervorgehen. Als Thorpe bunte Zuckerpapiere auszuschneiden und aufzukleben begann, um seinen selbst erlebten Stadtlandschaften das Aussehen vereinfachter Film-Stills zu verleihen, entdeckte er eine Methode, das von den weithin konsumierten Medienbildern gegebene Versprechen für sich einzulösen, das heißt, eine greifbare Verbindung aufzubauen zwischen deren imaginärer Welt und seinem Dasein in der Realzeit. Die akribisch ausgeschnittenen und aufgeklebten Bilder stellen phantastische Projektionen der Skyline Südwestlondons dar, wo er lebte, und blenden örtliche und massenkulturelle Bezugspunkte ineinander.

Indem er Verbindungen zwischen imaginierter und »vorgefundener« Bilderwelt herausformte, begann Thorpe mit seiner längerfristigen Auslotung des Schnittpunkts zwischen individuellem Handeln und der Welt als gegebener Entität.

Seine Collagen aus den mittleren und späten neunziger Jahren zeigten großdimensionierte Anlagen, die Vergnügungsmöglichkeiten boten – einige aufgrund von kreativem Einfallsreichtum seitens der Beteiligten, andere planmäßig. Schemenhafte Nachtlandschaften von Menschen auf Rummelplätzen und in Drahtseilbahnen standen neben Kompositionen mit konkreten architektonischen Strukturen, die von Stadtbewohnern zurückerobert wurden, und damit eine Form des *détournement* in der urbanen Landschaft darstellen. *Fun* präsentierte als riesige Klettergerüste imaginierte Masten, *Need for Speed* eine Autobahnüberführung als Aussichtsplatz für Sternschnuppen (beide 1997). Später wurde Thorpes Umgang mit seinen Materialien komplexer und näherte sich der ausgeprägten Schichtung, die in seinen 2004 bis 2006 entstandenen Bildern zu erkennen ist. Die Bildquellen verlagerten sich von der Stadtlandschaft zu eindrucksvollen Wildnissen mit darin eingefügten merkwürdigen Architekturstrukturen. In *Out from the Night the Day is Beautiful ...* (1999), auf der man einen Hängegleiter sieht, der sich vor den auf einer Berglandschaft aufragenden Kiefern abhebt, erzeugt das komplexe Arrangement kleiner Stückchen eine tarnmusterähnlich konturierte Oberfläche.

Der zunehmende Konstruktionsaufwand der Collagen, der eine Reihe neuer Materialien und eine Verdickung der Oberfläche mit sich bringt, könnte als Zeichen einer produktiven Rückbesinnung von Thorpes Praxis auf sich selbst gewertet werden. Neigte sein Projekt sich anfänglich einer unerreichbaren Bilderwelt zu – dem »Spektakel« der Massenkultur, wie sie sich in der allgemeinen Populärkultur darstellt –, so könnte der Künstler im Zuge der an dieser Stelle einsetzenden Entwicklung erkannt haben, was für endlose Möglichkeiten der Erfindung die Verarbeitung von Materialien selbst bietet. Die zwischen 2004 und 2006 entstandenen Collagen enthalten Papiertücher, getrocknete Rinde, massenproduzierten Schmuck, Schiefer, Glas und gepresste Gräser oder Blumen. Thorpes zusehends dichtere Installationen, wie etwa *The Colonist* (2004) oder *The Defeated Life Restored* (2007), veranschaulichen, in welchem Maße die Welt des Künstlers sich ausgedehnt hat: von einer Welt, die als zweidimensionales Bild darstellbar ist, zu einer, die den Saal in vier Dimensionen bespielt und als Kombination von Bildern, Skulpturen, Wandschirmen und handgemalten Plakaten mit poetischen Statements Gestalt annimmt.

Architekturelemente in Gestalt von Wandschirmen aus Holz und Glas, die den Raum, in dem die Zeichnungen, Skulpturen und Collagen gezeigt werden, markieren und gliedern, sind zum festen Bestandteil von Thorpes Ausstellungen geworden. Dies zeigt, wie sehr die »Welt« seines Werks nun für sich selber bestehen kann. Im Gegensatz zur zeitgenössischen Tradition des Reagierens auf örtliche Gegebenheiten prägt Thorpes Installationskonzept durch seine heraldische Beschaffenheit den Raum, in dem es ausgestellt ist, und setzt sich über dessen physikalische

Eigenschaften hinweg. Die mehr oder minder symmetrische Anlage von *The Defeated Life Restored* bekundet dies bislang am schärfsten, indem sie die Erfahrung des Zuschauers im Werk ablenkt vom Bewusstsein für die vorhandenen Architekturelemente – etwa die Anordnung von Türen und Fenstern – und die konventionellen weißen Flächen überdeckt mit Wandschirmen, die auf einem abgesteckten Raum beharren, der zur werkeigenen Gestalt, Textur und Musterung passt. Die innerhalb der Wandschirme aufgebauten drei mosaikartig gemusterten »Marschflugkörper«-Skulpturen weisen die Solidität und Dauerhaftigkeit architektonischer Säulen auf.

In Thorpes Installationen bilden die Objekte und Bilder komplexe Verkettungen, die der unterschwelligen Fiktion der Autarkie ein konkreteres Profil verleihen, indem sie auf Überlebensstrategien von Pionieren anspielen. Der allegorische Mehrwert zieht sich als roter Faden durch alle diese Konzeptionen hindurch. Die Skulpturen sind sowohl praktische Gegenstände, die in der Welt von Thorpes Landschaftsbildern auftreten könnten, als auch schlichte ästhetische Objekte. Ständige Maßstabsverlagerungen – von einem auf einer Collage dargestellten Haus über ein abstraktes Architekturmodell bis zum großformatigen Wandschirm – untergraben die Möglichkeit konkreter Momente realistischer Darstellung, die sich an einem vorhandenen Bezugspunkt festmachen ließen. Thorpes frühere Aquarelle schienen als »Musterexemplare« aus seiner natürlich-biologischen Anschauungswelt so etwas wie Wahrheit zu bieten. Doch genauer besehen, erwachsen diese Pflanzen aus und sind durchwirkt von den Geometrien der vom Menschen geschaffenen Kultur. In jüngeren Werken haben die Pflanzen ausgefeiltere Formen angenommen und erscheinen nun als ein Bausatz von Insignien, so als seien sie durch jene genetische Struktur kodiert, die eine potenzielle Anwendungsbasis für alle imaginativ erzeugten Vorhaben oder Pläne des Künstlers bildet, und zeugten gleichzeitig von einem Familienerbe.

Die Undurchdringlichkeit, für die Thorpes wehrhafte ornamentale Festung sorgt, lässt sich sicher auch als Kontrapunkt zu ihrer materiellen Zerbrechlichkeit auffassen. Sie veranschaulicht, dass dem Künstler die ungeheure Verletzlichkeit dieser Art von Schöpfung bewusst ist, die innerhalb der realen Ökonomie von Arbeit und Tausch als Insel einer Spezialistentätigkeit auftritt. Die akribische Oberflächenausgestaltung seiner Objekte veranschaulicht, dass die Freude am Handwerk in eine beinahe kontraproduktive Obsession umschlägt, und deutet auf Thorpes Bekenntnis zur Lage des Künstler-Werktätigen als einer luxuriösen und deshalb notgedrungen geschützten und leicht paranoiden Position. Thorpes Haltung zur »Arbeit« eröffnet eine andere Art von Zeit, als es die gemessene und durch die mechanisierte Regelmäßigkeit des Spätkapitalismus' beschleunigte Zeit ist. Die Bilder und Objekte, die er fertigt, sind langwierig und schwer verdaulich, weil sie die Taktung der Produktion und das Spektakel der Konsumgesellschaft unterbrechen. Die geheimnisvolle und verrätselnde Natur der zahlreichen hermetischen Bezugspunkte, die in die Geschichte zurückreichen und seitwärts in verschiedene Nischen der Subkultur hineingreifen, um dort nach materiellen Identifikationspunkten zu suchen, laufen den zeitgenössischen Vorstellungen einer »partizipatorischen« Praxis mit demokratischem Appeal zuwider. Vielmehr spricht das Werk eine zweischneidige Einladung aus und erwehrt sich zugleich der Gesellung, ganz ähnlich der Auffassung von Sun Ra, der seine Philosophie mit den Worten beschrieb, er »baue manchen eine Brücke, anderen eine Mauer«.

In *The Mighty Lights Community Project* (2003) inszenierte der Künstler ein imaginäres »Treffen« der Bewohner seiner Welt als Performance[10]. Die Mitwirkenden, die zueinander passende T-Shirts trugen, machten in Formation Scherensprünge und skandierten dabei für Thorpes Gedichte typische Hymnen und Gesänge über das auf schillernde Weise begeisternde und finstere Thema des utopischen Gemeinschaftslebens in einer geteilten, herrlichen Zukunft. Der allegorische Impuls in Thorpes Arbeit sorgt dafür, dass eine solche Phantasie der Gemeinschaftlichkeit die Existenz des Werks in jener Art menschlicher Begriffe erklärt, die der aktuelle Kunstdiskurs nicht zulässt. Durchwoben von Fiktion, kann das Werk geheimnisvoller, schöner, unverortbarer oder unentzifferbarer sein, als dies sonst, rational, möglich wäre. Wie in Thorpes Pflanzenexemplaren Entwürfe für Häuser »wachsen«, bringt die Fiktion seine Kunst zur Blüte. Im Unterschied zum frühmodernen Projekt der russischen Konstruktivisten beispielsweise, denen eine neue Welt vorschwebte, die durch ihre auf alles – von politischen Plakaten über die Kleidung der Arbeiter bis zur Innengestaltung – angewandten revolutionären abstrakten Designs zur Anerkennung durchstoßen sollte, erschafft Thorpe eine Welt, die, nebenbei, sowohl *Produkt* seiner Idealgemeinschaft als auch Blaupause ihres *Potenzials* ist. Sie vollzieht keinen radikalen oder kritisch-dekonstruktiven Bruch mit der Vergangenheit, sondern greift auf ihr Material zurück, um daraus einen Bausatz neuer ästhetischer Beziehungen und Positionen zu entwickeln.

[1] Gespräch mit Rainald Schumacher, in: Kat. d. Ausst. »Imagination Becomes Reality: Part III«, München (Sammlung Goetz) 2006, S. 176. [2] In einer Rezension zu Thorpes Ausstellung *The Colonists* in der Karlsruher Galerie Meyer Riegger 2004 habe ich festgehalten, dass er die Idee der »Kultivierung« im Sinne einer verballhornten Etymologie gebraucht, die »Kult und Kultur kombiniert«. Catherine Wood, »David Thorpe: Meyer Riegger, Karlsruhe«, in: *Frieze*, Nr. 84, Juni – August 2004. [3] In zwei Teilen erschienen in *October*, Ausgabe 12 und 13 (Frühjahr/Sommer 1980). [4] Ebenda, S. 64. [5] Ebenda, S. 85. [6] Gespräch mit Rainald Schumacher (wie Anm. 1). [7] David Thorpe, *The Kingdom of Seekers*, *Metropolis M*, Nr. 2, April/Mai 2004. [8] So formulierte ich in meinem Text zu Thorpes Ausstellung im Art Now Space, British Tate, London. [9] Craig Owens, "Beyond Recognition: Representation, Power, and Culture", 1994, S. 58. [10] Tate Britain, als Teil von Tate & Egg Live, 2003.

SELF EMPOWERMENT, HIGHER LIFE
AUTONOMY AND DEFEAT
A STUTTERING BY DANIEL BAUMANN
SELBSTBEFÄHIGUNG, HÖHERES LEBEN,
AUTONOMIE, SIEG UND NIEDERLAGE
GESTAMMELTE TEXTE VON DANIEL BAUMANN

A STUTTERING
DANIEL BAUMANN

THEODORE JOHN »TED« KACZYNSKI (born 1942), also known as the *Unabomber*, is an American anarchist best known for his campaign of mail bombs sent to several universities and airlines in the late 1970s and early 1990s, killing three and wounding 23. In *Industrial Society and Its Future* (commonly called the 'Unabomber Manifesto') he argued that his actions were a necessary (although extreme) ruse by which to attract attention to what he believed were the dangers of modern technology. Kaczynski did this in the hope that it would inspire others to fight against what he considered subjugation facilitated by technological progress. **SIMPLE LIVING** is a lifestyle individuals may pursue for a variety of motivations, such as spirituality, health, ecology, social justice or a rejection of consumerism. Its proponents are consciously choosing to not focus on wealth directly tied to money or cash-based economics. **OPEN SOURCE** describes the principles and methodologies promoting open access to the production and design processes of various goods, products and resources with relaxed intellectual property restrictions. **LARRY MCMURTRY** (born 1936) is an American born Academy Award winning screenwriter, novelist and essayist who purchased a rare book store in Washington D.C.'s Georgetown neighbourhood in 1970 and named it *Booked Up*. In 1988 he opened a second *Booked Up* in Archer City, establishing the town as an American 'Book City'. The Archer City store is arguably the largest used bookstore in the US, carrying over 400,000 titles. **EDWARD PAUL ABBEY** (1927-1989) was an author and essayist noted for his advocacy of environmental issues and criticism of public land policies. His best-known works include the novel *The Monkey Wrench Gang*, cited as an inspiration by radical environmental groups, and the non-fiction work *Desert Solitaire*. Larry McMurtry referred to Abbey as the "Thoreau of the American West". He differed from the stereotype of the "environmentalist as politically-correct leftist", by disclaiming the counterculture and "trendy campus people" and by supporting some conservative causes such as immigration reduction and the National Rifle Association. An innovative jazz composer, bandleader, piano and synthesizer player **SUN RA** (1914–1993) came to be known as much for his "cosmic philosophy" as for his musical compositions and performances. Claiming that he was of the 'Angel Race' and not from Earth, but from Saturn, Ra developed complicated 'cosmic' philosophies and lyrical poetry that preached 'awareness' and above all, peace. Some regarded him as a crank because of this, but most recognized his immense musical talent. **ALICE COLTRANE**, born Alice McLeod (1937–2007) was an American jazz pianist, organist, composer and one of the few harpists in the history of jazz. In the early 1970s, after years of involvement with Eastern religion, Coltrane took the name Swamini Turiyasangitananda. She was a devotee of the Indian guru Sathya Sai Baba. Isaac Tigrett, a prominent follower and co-founder of the Hard Rock Café, stated in the BBC documentary that his admiration for the Baba would not change even if the charges against Baba of paedophilia and murder were proved beyond all doubt. (*Secret Swami* BBC TV documentary, June 2004). **ALBERT AYLER** (1936–1970), a jazz saxophonist, singer and composer, was the most primal of the American free jazz

musicians of the 1960s. In 1966 Ayler was signed to *Impulse Records* at the urging of John Coltrane, the label's star attraction at that time. But even on *Impulse* Ayler's radically different music never found a sizable audience. In a letter to *The Cricket*, a Newark, New Jersey music magazine edited by Amiri Baraka and Larry Neal, Albert reported that he had seen a strange object in the sky and come to believe that he and his brother "had the right seal of God Almighty in our forehead". Peter Brötzmann's 'Die Like A Dog Quartet' is a group loosely dedicated to Ayler. **EDWARD CARPENTER** (1844–1929) was an English socialist poet, anthologist, and an early homosexual activist. Influenced by Henry Hyndman, he joined the Social Democratic Federation (SDF) in 1883 which became the Sheffield Socialist Society. In 1884, he left the SDF with William Morris to join the Socialist League. Increasingly attracted by a life close to nature, Carpenter moved in with tenant farmer Albert Fearnehough and his family in Bradway. Their partnership in many ways reflected Carpenter's cherished conviction that homosexual love had the power to subvert class boundaries. It was his belief that in the future homosexual people would be the cause of radical social change in the social conditions of man. It was then that Carpenter began to develop the crux of his Socialist politics; influenced by John Ruskin, he envisioned a utopian future that took the form of primitive communism which flatly rejected the industrialism of the Victorian age. During the 1880s, Carpenter developed an intellectual passion for Hindu mysticism and Indian philosophy. He received a pair of sandals from a friend in India, and began to manufacture them, on a small-scale. This was the first successful introduction of sandals to Britain. **DAVID HERBERT LAWRENCE** (1885-1930) was a controversial English writer whose prolific and diverse output included novels, short stories, poems, plays, essays, travel books, paintings, translations, literary criticism and personal letters. His collected works represent an extended reflection upon the dehumanizing effects of modernity and industrialisation. Lawrence confronts issues relating to emotional health and vitality, spontaneity, sexuality, and instinctive behaviour. Lawrence's unsettling opinions earned him many enemies and he endured persecution, censorship and misrepresentation of his creative work throughout the second half of his life, much of which spent in a voluntary exile he called his "savage pilgrimage". At the time of his death, his public reputation was that of a pornographer who had wasted his considerable talents. **NIKOLA TESLA** (1856-1943), a renowned Serbian-American inventor, physicist, mechanical and electrical engineer, is best known for his revolutionary research into electricity and magnetism in the late 19th and early 20th centuries. In the US, Tesla's fame rivalled that of any other inventor or scientist in history, but due to his eccentric personality and, at the time, unbelievable and sometimes bizarre claims about possible scientific and technological developments, Tesla was ultimately ostracized, regarded as a 'mad scientist'. The single strangest invention he proposed was probably his 'thought photography' machine. He reasoned that a thought, formed in the mind, created a corresponding image in the retina, and that the electrical data of this neural transmission could be read and recorded in a machine. The stored information could then be processed through an artificial

optic nerve and played back as visual patterns on a screen. **ADOLF WÖLFLI** (1864-1930) was interned in the Waldau mental asylum near Bern, Switzerland, in 1895. In prose, poetry, music, mathematical calculations and inventories, Wölfli developed the St. Adolf-Giant-Creation, a brave world with its private mythology, a new childhood and glorious future, a one-man utopia mirroring the world he lived in and was excluded from. In 1925 **CHARLES EPHRAIM BURCHFIELD** (1893-1967), an American watercolour painter, moved from Buffalo, NY to the adjacent suburb of West Seneca, spending the rest of his life in the rural neighbourhood of Gardenville. He is known for his visual commentaries on the effects of Industrialism on small town America as well as for his paintings of nature. "One of the most isolated and original phenomena in American art." (Alfred Barr, 1930). Today, his paintings could be qualified as 'psychedelic'. **CHARLES ROBERT ASHBEE** (1863–1942), the son of businessman and erotic bibliophile Henry Spencer Ashbee, was a designer and entrepreneur who famously moved his Guild of Handicraft from London's Mile End Road – described in the 1880s by Samuel Barnett as one of the 'worst districts in London' – to the quint-essential rural peacefulness of Chipping Campden in the Cotswolds in 1902. This was Ashbee's new 'City of the Sun', symbolising fitness, cooperation and communal effort in a place "touched by a magic wand centuries ago and remaining spellbound". (Algernon Gissing, c. 1890). **WILLIAM MORRIS** (1834–1896) was one of the principal founders of the British Arts and Crafts movement, a writer of poetry and fiction, and best known as a designer of wallpaper and patterned fabrics. Morris and his daughter May were amongst Britain's first socialists, working with Eleanor Marx and Engels to begin the socialist movement. In 1883, he joined the Social Democratic Federation, and in 1884 organised the breakaway *Socialist League*. Morris's book, *The Wood Beyond the World*, is considered to have heavily influenced C. S. Lewis's *Narnia* series, while J. R. R. Tolkien was inspired by Morris's reconstructions of early Germanic life in *The House of the Wolfings* and *The Roots of the Mountains*. Editor and fantasy scholar Lin Carter credits William Morris with starting the imaginary-world fantasy genre with *The Well at the World's End*, set neither in the past, the future, nor on another planet. An American author, pacifist, nature lover, tax resister and individualist anarchist, **HENRY DAVID THOREAU** (1817-1862) was an advocate of civil disobedience and a lifelong abolitionist, who dreamt of the world becoming a utopia. Though not commonly regarded as a Christian anarchist, his essay *Civil Disobedience* is accredited with inspiring some of Leo Tolstoy's ideas. The origin of the **DOUKHOBORS** dates back to 16th and 17th century Russia. The Doukhobors ("Spirit Wrestlers") are a radical Christian sect that maintained a belief in pacifism and a communal lifestyle, while rejecting secular government. In 1899, the Doukhobors fled repression in Tsarist Russia and migrated to Canada, mostly in the provinces of Saskatchewan and British Columbia. The funds for the trip were paid for by the Quakers and Russian novelist Leo Tolstoy. Canada was suggested to Tolstoy as a safe-haven for the Doukhobors by the anarchist Peter Kropotkin who, while on a speaking tour across the country, observed the religious tolerance experienced by the Mennonites. **THE LUDDITES** were a social movement of English textile workers in the early 1800s who protested – often by destroying textile machines – against the changes produced by the Industrial Revolution which they felt threatened their jobs. The movement, which began in 1811, was named after a mythical leader, Ned Ludd. Neo-luddism opposes technology, both in particular and in general. Since there is no self-described group of 'neo-luddites', it is not a political movement. On the other hand, when controversial issues arise, advocates of one policy or another tend to group and agglomerate their efforts to affect policy. As a result, an amalgamation of liberal, conservative and radical elements appear a cohesive, anti-technology, neo-luddite group. **FRANÇOIS MARIE CHARLES FOURIER** (1772-1837) was a French utopian socialist and philosopher. Fourier coined the word *féminisme* in 1837; thirty years earlier he had argued that the extension of women's rights was the general principle of all social progress. Fourier believed people would be better off living in communal societies rather than isolated, individual living. He developed the idea of the *phalanstère*, a community of 1,600 people where there would be private property but activities including eating and cooking would be communal. Fourier inspired the founding of the communist community called *La Reunion*, as well as several other communities within the USA, such as *North American Phalanx*. **LA REUNION** was a socialist utopian community formed in 1855 by French, Belgian, and Swiss colonists approximately three miles west of the present Reunion Arena and Reunion Tower in downtown Dallas, Texas, near the forks of the Trinity River. The first brewery and butcher shop in Dallas were established by former colonists from La Reunion. The **NORTH AMERICAN PHALANX (NAP)** was a secular Utopian community located in Red Bank, in Monmouth County, New Jersey. The NAP was based on the ideas of Charles Fourier, and lasted from 1841 to 1856. **BROOK FARM**, a transcendentalist Utopian experiment, was put into practice by transcendentalist former Unitarian minister George Ripley and his wife Sophia at a farm in West Roxbury, Massachusetts, at that time nine miles from Boston. The community (1841-1847) was inspired by the socialist concepts of Charles Fourier. Nathaniel Hawthorne was a founding member of Brook Farm and presented a fictionalized portrait of it in his novel, *The Blithedale Romance*. **WILLIAM BLAKE** (1757-1827), *The Garden of Love* // I went to the Garden of Love, / And saw what I never had seen: / A Chapel was built in the midst, / Where I used to play on the green. // And the gates of this Chapel were shut, / And "Thou shalt not" writ over the door; / So I turned to the Garden of Love, / That so many sweet flowers bore; // And I saw it was filled with graves, / And tombstones where flowers should be; / And Priests in black gowns were walking their rounds, / And binding with briers my joys and desires. **THE DIGGERS** were an English group, begun by Gerard Winstanley (1609-1676), an English Protestant religious reformer and political activist during the Protectorate of Oliver Cromwell. Their name came from a belief in economic equality based upon a specific passage in the *Book of Acts*. The Diggers attempted to reform by 'levelling' real property, the existing social order, with an agrarian lifestyle based upon their ideas for the creation of small egalitarian rural communities. They contended that if only the common people of England would

form themselves into self-supporting communes, there would be no place in such a society for the ruling classes. The State was to crush the Digger colonies whenever they arose. The Religious Society of Friends (commonly known as **QUAKERS**) began in England in the 17th century by people who were dissatisfied with the existing denominations and sects of Christianity. Since its beginnings in England, Quakerism has spread to other countries, such as Bolivia, Guatemala, Kenya, Peru, Cuba and the United States. The number of Quakers is relatively small, approximately 350,000 worldwide. Unlike other groups that emerged within Christianity, the Religious Society of Friends has little hierarchical structure and no creeds. The various branches have widely divergent beliefs and practices, but the central concept to many Friends may be the "Inner Light" or "that of God within" each of us. The **SEEKERS**, or Legatine-Arians as they were sometimes known, were a Protestant dissenting group that emerged around the 1620s, probably inspired by the preaching of three brothers – Walter, Thomas, and Bartholomew Legate. Arguably, they are best thought of as forerunners of the Quakers, with whom many of them subsequently merged. Seekers considered all organised churches of their day to be corrupt, and preferred to wait for God's revelation. The Seekers were not an organised religious group in any way that would be recognised today. They were shambolic, informal and localised. 'Membership' of a local Seekers assembly did not preclude membership of another sect. Indeed, Seekers shunned creeds and each assembly tended to embrace a broad spectrum of ideas. That said, there were a number of beliefs and practices that made the Seekers distinctive from the large number of nonconformist dissenting groups that emerged around the time of the Commonwealth of England. Most significant was their form of collective worship. **LAURENCE CLARKSON** (1615-1667) was the most outspoken and notorious of a loose collection of radical Protestants known as the **RANTERS**, regarded as heretical by the established Church of that period. Their central idea was pantheistic, that God is, essentially, in every creature. This led them to deny the authority of the Church, of scripture, of the current ministry and of services. Many Ranters seem to have rejected a belief in immortality and in a personal God, and in many ways they resemble the 14th century *Brethren of the Free Spirit*, and seem to have been regarded by the government of the time as a genuine threat to social order. Ranters were often associated with nudity, which they may have used as a form of social protest, as well as a symbol for abandoning earthly goods. Ranters were accused of antinomianism, fanaticism, and sexual immorality, and put in prison until they recanted. In the middle of the 19th century the name was often applied to the Primitive Methodists, with reference to their crude and often noisy preaching. More recently, the historian J. C. Davis has suggested that the Ranters did not exist at all. According to Davis, the Ranters were a myth created by conservatives in order to endorse traditional values by comparison with an unimaginably radical 'other'. **ABIEZER COPPE** (1619-1672) was one of the English Ranters and a writer of prophetic religious pamphlets. One of Coppe's major works is the *Fiery Flying Roll* (1649), a tirade against inequality and hypocrisy which vividly evokes the charged and visionary atmosphere that swept over England during

the civil war. While Coppe's views were unpopular with Royalists, they were equally disliked by Parliamentarians, and shortly after the *Fiery Flying Roll* was published, he was imprisoned at Newgate Prison, and the book burned. Like Lodowick Muggleton and the Diggers' leader Gerard Winstanley, Coppe combined an egalitarian social vision with an apocalyptic, religious one. *"Go up to London, to London, that great City, write, write, write. And behold I writ, and lo a hand was sent to me, and a roll of a book was within, which this fleshly hand would have put wings to, before the time. Whereupon it was snatcht out of my hand, & the Roll thrust into my mouth, and I eat it up, and filled my bowels with it, where it was bitter as worm-wood; and it lay broiling, and burning in my stomack, till I brought it forth in this forme"*. Abiezer Coppe, excerpt from the *Fiery Flying Roll*, (1649). **A STUTTERING** by Daniel Baumann with the help of Bruce Haines, David Thorpe and Wikipedia.

GESTAMMELTE TEXTE
DANIEL BAUMANN

THEODORE JOHN »TED« KACZYNSKI (1942) alias *Unabomber*, ein für seine Briefbombenattentate berüchtigter amerikanischer Anarchist, schickte in den späten siebziger und frühen neunziger Jahren mehreren Universitäten und Fluggesellschaften Bomben, die drei Todesopfer und 23 Verletzte forderten. Im »Unabomber-Manifest« *Industrial Society and Its Future* bezeichnete er seine Aktionen als zwar extreme, aber notwendige List, um auf die Gefahren der modernen Technik aufmerksam zu machen. Kaczynski hoffte, damit auch andere für den Kampf gegen die von ihm diagnostizierte Unterdrückung durch den technischen Fortschritt anzuregen. **SIMPLE LIVING** ist ein Lebensstil, den man sich aus Gründen der Spiritualität, Gesundheit, Ökologie, sozialen Gerechtigkeit oder Konsumverweigerung zu eigen machen kann. Seine Verfechter sehen bewusst von geldlichem oder materiellem Wohlstand ab. **OPEN SOURCE** beschreibt die Grundlagen und Methoden der Förderung des offenen Zugangs zur Entwicklung und Herstellung von Gütern, Erzeugnissen und Ressourcen unter gelockerten Urheberrechtsbestimmungen. **LARRY MCMURTRY** (1936), mit dem Academy Award ausgezeichneter amerikanischer Drehbuchautor, Romancier und Essayist, erwarb 1970 einen Raritätenbuchladen, den er *Booked Up* nannte. 1988 eröffnete er in Archer City, die er als amerikanische »Book City« etablierte, ein zweites *Booked Up*, das mit 400.000 Titeln das wohl größte Buchantiquariat in den USA darstellt. **EDWARD PAUL ABBEY** (1927-1989) machte sich als Schriftsteller und Essayist mit seinem Engagement für die Umwelt und seiner Kritik an der staatlichen Bodenpolitik einen Namen. Zu seinen bekanntesten Werken zählen der Roman *The Monkey Wrench Gang*, auf den sich radikale Umweltgruppen berufen, und das Sachbuch *Desert Solitaire*. Der Schriftsteller Larry McMurtry bezeichnete Abbey als »Thoreau des amerikanischen Westens«. Vom Klischee des »Umweltschützers als politisch korrektem Linken« wich er ab, indem er Gegenkultur und »trendiges Campusvolk« verwarf und konservative Anliegen wie Einwanderungsbeschränkung sowie die National Rifle Association unterstützte. Der innovative Jazzkomponist, Bandleader, Klavier- und Synthesizerspieler **SUN RA** (1914?-1993) wurde für seine »kosmische Philosophie« ebenso bekannt wie für seine Musikkompositionen und -aufführungen. Ra behauptete, er entstamme einem »Engelsgeschlecht« und sei vom Saturn, nicht von der Erde. Dabei schuf er komplizierte »kosmische« Philosophien und lyrische Gedichte, die »Bewusstsein« und vor allem Frieden predigten. Manche hielten ihn deshalb für eine Spinner, doch die meisten erkannten sein überragendes musikalisches Talent an. **ALICE COLTRANE**, geborene Alice McLeod (1937-2007), war eine amerikanische Jazzpianistin, Organistin und eine der wenigen Harfenist(inn)en in der Geschichte des Jazz. Nach langjähriger Beschäftigung mit östlicher Religion nahm sie den Namen Swamini Turiyasangitananda an. Sie war eine Anhängerin des indischen Gurus Sathya Sai Baba. Isaac Tigrett, prominenter Fan und Mitgründer des Hard Rock Café, erklärte in einer Fernsehdokumentation der BBC, an ihrer Bewunderung für Baba hätte sich auch dann nichts geändert, wenn die gegen ihn erhobenen Anschuldigen wegen Pädophilie und Mordes zweifelsfrei erwiesen gewesen wären (*Secret Swami*, BBC, Juni 2004). **ALBERT AYLER** (1936–1970), Jazzsaxophonist, Sänger und Komponist, war der Urvater der amerikanischen Freejazzmusiker der sechziger Jahre. 1966 nahm ihn *Impulse Records* unter Vertrag, wofür sich John Coltrane, der damalige Star des Labels, eingesetzt hatte. Doch selbst auf *Impulse* fand radikal andere Musik kein nennenswertes Publikum. In einem Brief an das von Amiri Baraka und Larry Neal in Newark, New Jersey, herausgegebene Musikmagazin *The Cricket* berichtete Albert, er habe ein seltsames Objekt am Himmel gesichtet und glaube, er und sein Bruder trügen »das richtige Siegel des Allmächtigen auf der Stirn«. Peter Brötzmanns »Die Like A Dog Quartet« bezieht sich im weiteren Sinn auf Ayler. Der Engländer **EDWARD CARPENTER** (1844-1929) war ein sozialistischer Dichter, Herausgeber von Anthologien und früher Homosexuellenaktivist. Unter dem Einfluss von Henry Hyndman trat er 1883 der Social Democratic Federation (SDF) bei, aus der später die Sheffield Socialist Society hervorging. 1884 verließ er gemeinsam mit William Morris die SDF und schloss sich der Socialist League an. Zunehmend an naturnahem Leben orientiert, zog er zu dem Pachtbauern Albert Fearnehough und dessen Familie in Bradway. Die Partnerschaft mit ihm spiegelte in vieler Hinsicht Carpenters innige Überzeugung, dass in der Macht homosexueller Liebe, Klassenschranken zu überwinden. Er glaubte daran, dass in Zukunft Homosexuelle einen radikalen Wandel in den gesellschaftlichen Verhältnissen des Menschen bewirken würden. Damals entwickelte Carpenter den Kerngedanken seines sozialistischen Gesellschaftsentwurfs; von John Ruskin beeinflusst, stellte er sich eine utopische Zukunft in Form eines ursprünglichen Kommunismus vor, der dem Industrialismus der viktorianischen Ära eine Absage erteilte. In den 1880er Jahren entwickelte Carpenter eine geistige Leidenschaft für Hindu-Mystik und indische Philosophie. Von einem Freund in Indien bekam er ein Paar Sandalen geschenkt und begann, diese in kleiner Zahl herzustellen, womit er das Schuhwerk erfolgreich in Großbritannien einführte. **DAVID HERBERT LAWRENCE** (1885-1930) war ein umstrittener englischer Schriftsteller, dessen umfangreiche und vielgestaltige Produktion Romane, Kurzgeschichten, Gedichte, Dramen, Essays, Reisebeschreibungen, Gemälde, Übersetzungen, Literaturkritiken und persönliche Briefe umfasst. Lawrence setzte sich auseinander mit Fragen der emotionalen Gesundheit und Lebenskraft, mit Spontaneität, Sexualität und Triebverhalten. Mit seinen beunruhigenden Ansichten machte Lawrence sich viele Feinde, und in der zweiten Hälfte seines Lebens, von der er einen Großteil im freiwilligen Exil verbrachte, das er seine »wilde Pilgerfahrt« nannte, war er Verfolgung, Zensur und verfälschenden Darstellungen seines Schaffens ausgesetzt. Zum Zeitpunkt seines Todes galt er als Pornograph, der seine beträchtlichen Talente verschwendet hatte. **NIKOLA TESLA** (1856-1943), ein namhafter serbisch-amerikanischer Erfinder, Physiker, Maschinenbau- und Elektroingenieur, wurde berühmt für seine revolutionäre Elektrizitäts- und Magnetikforschung im späten 19. und frühen 20. Jahrhundert. In den USA genoss Tesla ebenso großen Ruhm wie jeder andere Erfinder oder Wissenschaftler in der Geschichte, doch aufgrund seiner exzentrischen Persönlichkeit und seinen für die damalige Zeit unglaublichen, ja zuweilen absonderlichen Thesen über mögliche wissenschaftliche und technologische Entwicklungen wurde er am Ende als Verrückter gebrandmarkt. Die allermerkwürdigste Erfindung, die er vorschlug, war wohl sein »Gedankenphotoapparat«. Er nahm an, ein im Bewusstsein formulierter Gedanke erzeuge ein Abbild auf der Netzhaut, so dass die elektrischen Daten dieser neuralen Übertragung sich mit Hilfe einer Maschine lesen und aufzeichnen lassen. Die gespeicherte Information ließe sich dann mit einem künstlichen Sehnerv verarbeiten und als optisches Muster auf einen Bildschirm überspielen. **ADOLF WÖLFLI** (1864-1930) wurde 1895 in die Psychiatrische Klinik Waldau nahe dem schweizerischen Bern eingewiesen. In Prosatexten, Gedichten, Musik, mathematischen Berechnungen und Bestandsverzeichnissen entwickelte er die Skt-Adolf-Riesen-Schöpfung, eine schöne Welt mit seiner privaten Mythologie, einer neuen Kindheit und herrlichen Zukunft. Diese Ein-Mann-Utopie spiegelte die Welt, in der er lebte und von der er ausgeschlossen war. 1925 zog der amerikanische Aquarellmaler **CHARLES EPHRAIM BURCHFIELD** (1893-1967) von Buffalo, NY, in die angrenzende Vorstadt West Seneca und verbrachte den Rest seines Lebens in der ländlichen Gegend des Weilers Gardenville. Er ist bekannt für seine visuellen Kommentare zu den Auswirkungen des Industrialismus auf das kleinstädtische Amerika sowie für seine Naturgemälde. »Eines der der einmaligen Phänomene in der amerikanischen Kunst und eines der orginellsten dazu« (Alfred Barr, 1930). **CHARLES ROBERT ASHBEE** (1863-1942), Sohn des Geschäftsmanns und Liebhabers erotischer Literatur Henry Spencer Ashbee, war ein Gestalter und Unternehmer, der seine Guild of Handicraft bekanntermaßen 1902 aus der Londoner Mile End Road – die Samuel Barnett in den 1880er Jahren als einen der übelsten Stadtbezirke beschrieb – in die ausgesprochen ländliche Friedsamkeit von Chipping Campden in den Cotswolds verlegte. Ashbees neuer »Sonnenstaat« symbolisierte Ertüchtigung, Genossenschaftlichkeit und gemeinsames Streben an einem Ort, »der vor Jahrhunderten von einem Zauberstab berührt wurde und noch immer verwunschen ist« (Algernon Gissing, um 1890). **WILLIAM MORRIS** (1834-1896) gehörte zu den wichtigsten Mitbegründern der britischen Arts-and-Crafts-Bewegung, schrieb Gedichte und erzählende Prosa und wurde berühmt mit seinen Entwürfen für Tapeten und gemusterte Stoffe. Morris und seine Tochter May zählten zu den ersten Sozialisten in Großbritannien und brachten mit Eleanor Marx und Friedrich Engels die sozialistische Bewegung auf den Weg. 1883 trat er der Social Democratic Federation bei und organisierte 1884 die sich davon abspaltende *Socialist League*. Morris' Buch *The Wood Beyond the World* soll maßgeblich Einfluss auf C.S. Lewis' Kinderbuchserie *Narnia* ausgeübt haben, während J.R.R. Tolkien sich von Morris' Rekonstruktionen frühgermanischen Lebens in *The House of the Wolfings* und *The Roots of the Mountains* anregen ließ. Laut der Verlegerin und Fantasy-Expertin Lin Carter hat William Morris die Gattung der in imaginären Welten angesiedelten phantastischen Literatur eingeleitet mit seinem Buch *The Well at the World's End*, das weder in der Vergangenheit noch in der Zukunft noch auf einem anderen

Planeten spielt. Der amerikanische Autor, Pazifist, Naturfreund, Steuerverweigerer und individualistische Anarchist **HENRY DAVID THOREAU** (1817-1862) war ein Verfechter zivilen Ungehorsams und der Sklavenbefreiung zeit seines Lebens, der davon träumte, dass die Welt zu Utopia würde. Obwohl er für gewöhnlich nicht zu den christlichen Anarchisten gerechnet wird, soll sein Essay *Civil Desobedience* in manchen Gedanken Tolstois Niederschlag gefunden haben. Die Anfänge der **DOUKHOBORS** liegen im Russland des 16. und 17. Jahrhunderts. Die Doukhobors (»Kämpfer im Geiste«) sind eine radikale christliche Sekte mit pazifistischer Gesinnung und kommunenartiger Lebensform, die jedoch weltliche Regierungen ablehnt. 1899 flohen sie vor der Verfolgung im zaristischen Russland und wanderten nach Kanada aus, wo sie sich vor allem in den Provinzen Saskatchewan und British Columbia ansiedelten. Die Kosten für die Überfahrt zahlten die Quäker und der russische Romanschriftsteller Leo Tolstoi. Auf Kanada als sicheren Hafen für die Doukhobors hatte Tolstoi der Anarchist Peter Kropotkin aufmerksam gemacht, der auf einer landesweiten Vortragsreise beobachtet hatte, welche religiöse Toleranz die Mennoniten erfuhren. **LUDDITES** waren eine soziale Bewegung englischer Textilarbeiter zu Anfang des 18. Jahrhunderts, die gegen die von der Industriellen Revolution ausgelösten Veränderungen protestierten – durch Zerstörung der mechanischen Webstühle –, da sie durch diese ihre Arbeitsplätze bedroht sahen. Die 1811 einsetzende Bewegung wurde nach ihrem sagenumwobenen Anführer Ned Ludd benannt. Der Neo-Luddismus richtet sich gegen jegliche Technologie im Besonderen wie im Allgemeinen. Da es keine selbstdefinierte Gruppe von »Neo-Luddites« gibt, handelt es sich nicht um eine politische Bewegung. Andererseits machen, wenn Streitfragen aufkommen, Vertreter unterschiedlicher politischer Auffassungen gemeinsame Sache, um Einfluss auf die Politik zu nehmen. So stellt sich in Endeffekt eine Vereinigung liberaler, konservativer und radikaler Elemente als neo-ludditische Anti-Technik-Front dar. **FRANÇOIS MARIE CHARLES FOURIER** (1772-1837) war ein französischer utopischer Sozialist und Philosoph. Fourier prägte 1837 den Begriff *féminisme*; bereits dreißig Jahre zuvor hatte er argumentiert, die Ausweitung der Frauenrechte sei das allgemeine Prinzip jeglichen Fortschritts. Nach seiner Auffassung stünden die Menschen besser da, wenn sie in kommunalen Gesellschaften lebten anstatt in individueller Isolation. Er entwickelte die Idee der *phalanstère*, einer Kommune von 1600 Personen, in der es Privateigentum gäbe, doch zum Beispiel Essen und Kochen Gemeinschaftssache wäre. Fourier inspirierte zur Gründung der kommunistischen Kommune *La Reunion* sowie anderer Kommunen in den USA, etwa der *North American Phalanx*. Französische, belgische und schweizerische Siedler gründeten 1855 die utopische sozialistische Gemeinschaft **LA REUNION** ungefähr drei Meilen westlich der heutigen Reunion Arena bzw. Reunion Tower im Stadtzentrum von Dallas, Texas, nahe der Gabelung des Trinity River. Die erste Brauerei und die erste Metzgerei in Dallas wurden von früheren La-Reunion-Kolonisten gegründet. Die **NORTH AMERICAN PHALANX (NAP)** war eine weltliche utopische Gemeinschaft mit Sitz in Red Bank, Monmouth Country, New Jersey. Die NAP beruhte auf den Ideen Charles Fouriers und bestand von 1841 bis 1856. **BROOK FARM**, ein utopisches Experiment transzendentalistischer Prägung, wurde ins Leben gerufen von dem ehemaligen unitarischen Geistlichen George Ripley und dessen Frau Sophia auf einem Bauernhof in West Roxbury, Massachusetts, damals neun Meilen von Boston entfernt. Die Kommune (1841-1847) war inspiriert von den sozialistischen Konzepten Charles Fouriers. Nathaniel Hawthorne zählte zu den Gründungsmitgliedern von Brook Farm und setzte ihr ein literarisches Denkmal in seinem Roman *The Blithedale Romance*. **WILLIAM BLAKE** (1757-1827), *Der Garten der Liebe //* Ich ging in den Garten der Liebe / Und sah, was ich niemals geschaut: / Eine Kirche war, wo im Grünen / Als Kind ich einst spielte, gebaut. // Und die Pforten waren verschlossen, / Du sollst nicht stand über der Tür; / So wandte ich mich zum Garten / Und suchte nach Blumen wie früh'r. // Statt Blumen fand ich dort Gräber / Und Grabsteine um sie herum / Gingen Priester in Scharen in schwarzen Talaren, // Die spießten mit Stangen mein Glück und Verlangen. Die englische Gruppe **THE DIGGERS** wurde in der Zeit des Protektorats Oliver Cromwells gegründet von Gerard Winstanley (1609-1676), einem englischen Protestanten, Religionsreformer und politischen Aktivisten. Der Name beruht auf dem Glauben an ökonomische Gleichheit, der aus einer bestimmten Stelle im *Buch der Taten* (Apostelgeschichte) hervorgeht. Die Diggers versuchten die bestehende Gesellschaftsordnung durch »Angleichung« des Grundvermögens zu reformieren und pflegten einen agrarischen Lebensstil, der auf ihren Ideen zur Einrichtung egalitärer kleiner Landkommunen fußte. Nach ihrer Auffassung brauchte das einfache Volk Englands nur in selbst tragenden Kommunen zu organisieren, damit in einer solchen Gesellschaft kein Platz mehr für die herrschenden Klassen wäre. Wann immer sie auftauchten, wurden die Digger-Siedlungen vom Staat zerschlagen. Die Religiöse Gesellschaft der Freunde (allgemein **QUÄKER** genannt), entstand im 17. Jahrhundert in England aus Unzufriedenheit mit den bestehenden Konfessionen und Sekten des Christentums. Seit seinen Anfängen in England hat das Quäkertum sich in anderen Ländern, wie Bolivien, Guatemala, Kenia, Peru, Kuba und den USA, verbreitet. Verhältnismäßig gering an Zahl, gibt es weltweit etwa 350.000 Quäker. Im Unterschied zu anderen Gruppen, die sich aus dem Christentum herausgelöst haben, kennt die Religiöse Gesellschaft der Freunde kaum hierarchische Strukturen und keine Glaubensbekenntnisse. Die einzelnen Zweige haben weitgehend unterschiedliche Glaubensformen und Gepflogenheiten, doch die Kernvorstellung vieler Quäker ist möglicherweise die des »Inneren Lichts« oder dass »Gott in jedem von uns« ist. Die **SEEKERS** oder Legatine-Arians, wie sie manchmal heißen, waren eine protestantische Abweichlergruppe, die um 1620 entstand, und zwar wahrscheinlich aus dem Geiste der Predigten dreier Brüder: Walter, Thomas und Bartholomew Legate. Sie sind vermutlich als Vorläufer der Quäker zu begreifen, mit denen viele von ihnen sich später vermischten. Die Seekers betrachteten alle Amtskirchen ihrer Zeit als korrupt und zogen es vor, auf die Offenbarung Gottes zu warten. Sie bildeten keine organisierte Religionsgemeinschaft der Art, wie sie heute anerkannt würde, sondern agierten anarchisch, informell und ortsbezogen. Die »Mitgliedschaft« in einer Ortsversammlung der Seekers schloss die Mitgliedschaft in einer anderen Sekte nicht aus. So mieden sie Glaubensbekenntnisse und ließen in ihren Versammlungen ein breites Ideenspektrum zu. Mit einigen Überzeugungen und Gepflogenheiten zeichneten sich die Seekers jedoch gegenüber den zahlreichen nonkonformen Splittergruppen aus, die zur Zeit des Commonwealth in England entstanden. Besonders charakteristisch war ihre Form kollektiver Andacht. **LAURENCE CLARKSON** (1615-1667) war der freimütigste und namhafteste Vertreter eines losen Zusammenschlusses radikaler Protestanten, die als **RANTERS** bekannt sind und von der damaligen Amtskirche als Ketzer betrachtet wurden. Ihr Kerngedanke war ein pantheistischer, das heißt, dass Gott dem Wesen nach in jedem Geschöpf ist. Deshalb lehnten sie die Autorität der Kirche und der Schriften ebenso ab wie die der gängigen Geistlichkeit und Liturgie. Viele Ranters verweigerten wohl auch den Glauben an die Unsterblichkeit und an einen persönlichen Gott, womit sie in mancher Hinsicht den *Brüder vom freien Geiste* aus dem 14. Jahrhundert ähneln. Die Ranters galten bei der damaligen Regierung als echte Bedrohung der Gesellschaftsordnung. Oft werden sie mit Nacktheit in Verbindung gebracht, die möglicherweise eine Form des sozialen Protests und ein Symbol zur Lösung von irdischen Gütern darstellte. Des Antinomianismus, Fanatismus und der sexuellen Unsittlichkeit bezichtigt, wurden die Ranters ins Gefängnis gesteckt, bis sie widerriefen. Mitte des 19. Jahrhunderts wandte man den Namen häufig auf die Primitive Methodists an – wegen deren ungehobelter und oftmals lärmender Predigten. In jüngerer Zeit vertrat der Historiker J.C. Davis die These, die Ranters habe es nie gegeben, sondern sie seien ein von Konservativen aufgebrachter Mythos, um die traditionellen Werte durch Entgegensetzung eines unvorstellbar radikalen »Anderen« zu untermauern. **ABIEZER COPPE** (1619-1672) war einer der englischen Ranters und Verfasser prophetischer religiöser Streitschriften. Zu seinen Hauptwerken zählt *Fiery Flying Roll* (1649), eine Tirade gegen Ungleichheit und Heuchelei, die das spannungsgeladene und visionäre Klima evoziert, das während des Bürgerkriegs über England hereinbrach. Coppes Ansichten waren bei Royalisten ebenso unbeliebt wie bei den Parlamentaristen verpönt, und kurz nach dem Erscheinen von *Fiery Flying Roll* wurde der Autor im Newgate Prison inhaftiert und das Buch verbrannt. Wie Lodowick Muggleton und das Oberhaupt der Diggers, Gerard Winstanley, verband Coppe eine egalitäre Gesellschaftsvision mit einer apokalyptischen, religiösen Prophezeiung. »Zieh nach London, nach London, der großen Stadt, schreib, schreib, schreib. Und wie ich schrieb, siehe, da ward mir eine Hand gesandt, und darinnen war eine Rolle aus einem Buch, welcher diese fleischliche Hand vor Zeiten mag Flügel verliehen haben. Darob wurde sie mir aus der Hand gerissen & die Rolle mir in den Mund gestoßen, und ich aß sie auf und füllte meine Eingeweide damit, wo sie bitter war wie Wermut; und sie lag sengend und brennend mir im Magen, bis ich sie dieser Gestalt hervorgebracht.« Abiezer Coppe, Auszug aus *Fiery Flying Roll* (1649). **GESTAMMELTE TEXTE** von Daniel Baumann, unter Mitwirkung von Bruce Haines, David Thorpe und Wikipedia.

THE INNER LIGHT

THE INNER LIGHT, THE INNER LIGHT

THE INNER LIGHT IS WITHIN ME

THE INNER LIGHT IS WITHIN ME

The Inner Light, The Inner Light

ECSTASY IS HERE

ECSTASY IS HERE

THE INNER LIGHT IS WITHIN ME

THE INNER LIGHT IS WITHIN ME

You Are Nothing

YOU ARE NOTHING

Ecstasy is here

ECSTASY IS HERE

GO!

This World Is Not For You

This World Is Not For You

YOU ARE NOTHING

YOU ARE NOTHING

GO!

THE DEFEATED WORLD IS WITHIN ME

THE DEFEATED WORLD IS WITHIN ME

This World Is Not for You

THIS WORLD IS NOT FOR YOU

GO!

ECSTASY IS HERE

ECSTASY IS HERE

THE INNER LIGHT IS WITHIN ME

THE INNER LIGHT IS WITHIN ME

THE INNER LIGHT, THE INNER LIGHT

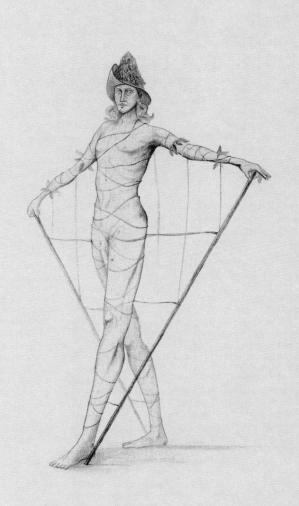

Howle Howle

Ye Great Ones!
As I Whoope Whoope
AND SING SING!
CONQUERED AM I
BY MY TRUE MAJESTY,
BY MY JUBILANT MARCH,
BY MY GREAT GREAT TYRANNY,
BY MY HOSTILE ACTS,
BY MY BESIEGED AND BEWILDERED SELF
BY MY

SPLENDOUR!

MY

SPLENDOUR!

By My Embarked Upon Strange
And Solitary Deeds,
BY MY GREAT GREAT TREACHERY,
BY MY COMMUNITY, IN ME!
My Beauty, In Me!
My Love, In Me!
By My Shelter,
MY GLORY, MY GLORY!
Howle Howle, Ye Great Ones
AS I WHOOPE WHOOPE
AND SING SING!
In Joy
AT MY GREAT CAPTIVITY!

MY DEAR HEARTS
MY DOVES
MY SWEET ONES
MY LOVES
I OFFER YOU A
GIFT
OF A GLIMPSE,
A Kiss
Through the fog,
A PIERCING,
A CUT,
a Crack through the Rock,
A LIGHT
SHINING
But briefly
THAT BLINDS
THEN BURNS
THEN FLEES FROM YOU.
Yes I offer you
My Dear Ones
A WHISPER AND A HINT
Of a Life that Shines
Of a Life that Glows
Of my Life that Sparkles
Of my Life as Gold
THE UNIVERSE AS MINE!
THE UNIVERSE AS MINE!
FOR I LIVE A LIFE OF A
LOVE
RESTORED!

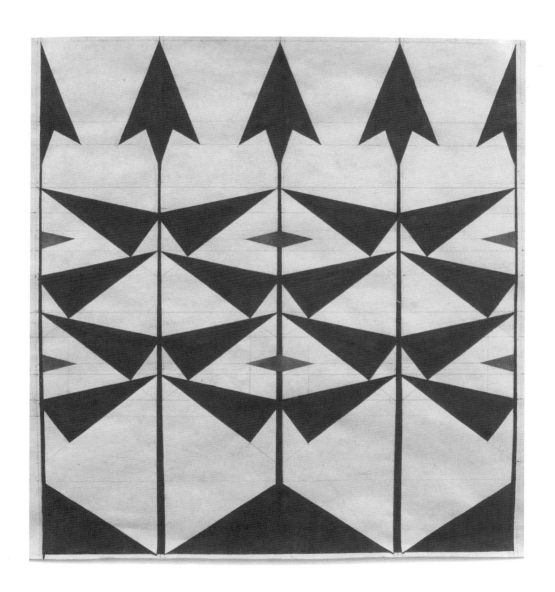

I Am Jubilant
I Am Jubilant
I AM JUBILANT IN MY DEFEAT
I AM JUBILANT IN MY DEFEAT
For I Have Seen My Land
I Have Seen My Land
My Beautiful Land
My Peaceable Land
FOR MY LAND IS AS LIGHT
MY LAND IS AS LIGHT
CONCEALED FROM YOU
Concealed From You
For I Retreat, I Retreat, I Retreat
To My Land
I March To My Land
My Peaceable Land
FOR MY LAND IS AS LIGHT!
MY LAND IS AS LIGHT!
HIDDEN FROM YOU
Hidden From You
For I Am Dressed In My Land
Cloaked In My Land
YOUR SHADOWS MY LAND
YOUR SHADOWS MY LAND
I Retreat, I Retreat, I Retreat
To My Land.
FOR YOUR LIGHT IS FINISHED!
YOUR LIGHT IS FINISHED!
FOR I AM GLORY TURNED
AGAINST YOU

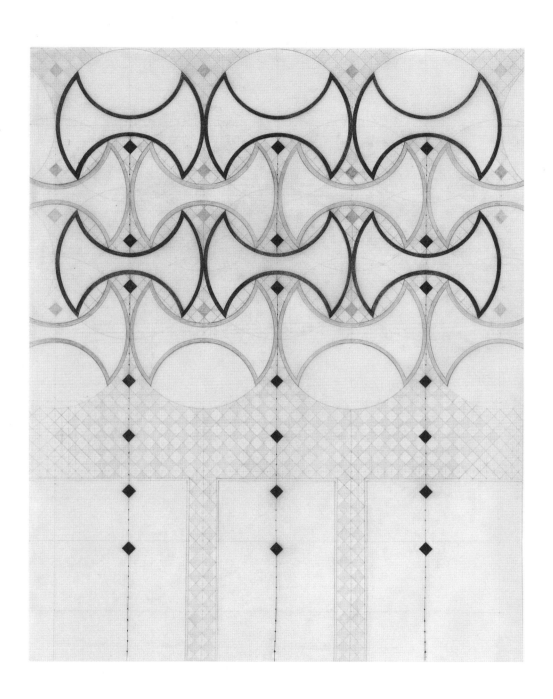

HAIL, HAIL
The Broken Seed,
The Great Castaway,
The Fragile Wreck,
The Scattered And Banished Root,
Cast Out!
THE EXILED FLOWER
Sprang Forth
Blossoming!
THE RUIN OF YOU ALL!
THE RUIN OF YOU ALL!
The Dying Fruit Gathered,
AS BOUNTY,
Blossoming!
An Island, In Shadows,
IN SHELTER,
Blossoming!
The Ripe Fruit Turned Fleshly,
IN DARKNESS,
Blossoming!
Hail, Hail, The Broken Seed,
The Great Castaway,
The Banished Root,
THE RUIN OF YOU ALL!
THE RUIN OF YOU ALL!
The Exiled Flower,
IN DARKNESS,
Blossoming!

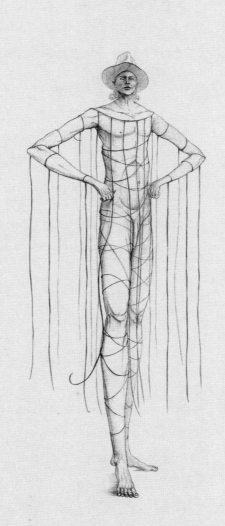

THE DEFEATED LIFE RESTORED is published to accompany an exhibition by David Thorpe *The Defeated Life Restored*, organised by Camden Arts Centre with Kunsthaus Glarus and Museum Kurhaus Kleve.

EXHIBITION SCHEDULE
Kunsthaus Glarus, 4 February – 15 April 2007
Camden Arts Centre, London 27 April – 1 July 2007
Museum Kurhaus Kleve, 25 November 2007 –
17 February 2008

Kunsthaus Glarus, Im Volksgarten, Postfach 665
CH-8750 Glarus, Switzerland T: +41 55 640 25 35
www.kunsthausglarus.ch
Camden Arts Centre, Arkwright Road, London
NW3 6DG, England T: +44 (0)20 7472 5500
www.camdenartscentre.org
Museum Kurhaus Kleve, Tiergartenstraße 41,
D-47533 Kleve, Germany T: +49 2821 75010
www.museumkurhaus.de

ISBN 978 1 900470 64 3. **EDITION** 1000 copies. **EDITED BY** Bruce Haines. **DESIGNED BY** John and Orna Designs. **TRANSLATION** Stefan Barmann. **INSTALLATION PHOTOGRAPHY AT KUNSTHAUS GLARUS** A. Burger. **COPYRIGHT** © David Thorpe, the authors and Camden Arts Centre. Reproductions of artworks courtesy the artist and Maureen Paley, London, Meyer Riegger, Karlsruhe and 303 Gallery, New York © the artist. The exhibition is supported by the Stanley Thomas Johnson Foundation and the Henry Moore Foundation.

PUBLISHED BY CAMDEN ARTS CENTRE 2007 Registered charity 1065829/0. Registered company 2947191. **REGISTERED OFFICE** Arkwright Road, London, NW3 6DG. VAT reg. no 586 9041 03. All rights reserved. No part of this publication may be reproduced, stored in a retrieval system, transmitted in any form or by any means electronic, mechanical, including photocopying, recording or otherwise, without prior permission in writing from the publisher. All efforts have been made to trace copyright holders. Any errors or omissions will be corrected in subsequent editions if notification is given in writing to the publishers.

ACKNOWLEDGEMENTS David Thorpe would like to thank: Jenni Lomax and Bruce Haines, Camden Arts Centre. Nadia Schneider, Kunsthaus Glarus. Dr. Roland Mönig, Museum Kurhaus Kleve. Catherine Wood, Tate, London. Daniel Baumann, Adolf Wölfli Foundation, Museum of Fine Arts Bern. Maureen Paley, Maureen Paley, London. Thomas Riegger and Jochim Meyer, Meyer Riegger, Karlsruhe. Lisa Spellman, 303 Gallery, New York. Susan Stoops, Worcester Art Museum, Massachusetts. Victoria Adam, Ruth Proctor, Peter Linde Busk, Nick Byrnes, Katherine Gould, Anthea Hamilton, Andrew Palmer, Sara Knowland, James McCann, Joe Walsh, Paul Richards, Hannah Brown, Henna Vainio, Francis Taylor, Emily, Daphne, Dan Davies, Ranko Andjelic, Torbien Anderson, Tomoya Matsuzaki, Nick Sawyer, Norma and Ronald Thorpe. **DEDICATED TO** Marie Torbensdatter Hermann.

THE DEFEATED LIFE RESTORED Publikation aus Anlass der Ausstellung: David Thorpe *The Defeated Life Restored*, organisiert vom Camden Arts Centre in Kooperation mit dem Kunsthaus Glarus und dem Museum Kurhaus Kleve.

AUSSTELLUNGSSTATIONEN UND -DATEN
Kunsthaus Glarus, 4. Februar – 15. April 2007
Camden Arts Centre, London 27. April – 1. Juli 2007
Museum Kurhaus Kleve, 25. November 2007 –
17. Februar 2008

Kunsthaus Glarus, Im Volksgarten, Postfach 665
CH-8750 Glarus, Schweiz T: +41 55 640 25 35
www.kunsthausglarus.ch
Camden Arts Centre, Arkwright Road, London
NW3 6DG, England T: +44 (0)20 7472 5500
www.camdenartscentre.org
Museum Kurhaus Kleve, Tiergartenstraße 41,
D-47533 Kleve, Deutschland T: +49 2821 75010
www.museumkurhaus.de

ISBN 978 1 900470 64 3. **AUFLAGE** 1000 Exemplare. **REDAKTION** Bruce Haines. **GESTALTUNG** John and Orna Designs. **ÜBERSETZUNG** Stefan Barmann. **AUSSTELLUNGSPHOTOGRAPHIE IM KUNSTHAUS GLARUS** A. Burger. **COPYRIGHT** © David Thorpe, die Autoren und Camden Arts Centre. Abbildungen der Arbeiten von David Thorpe, Courtesy Maureen Paley, London, Meyer Riegger, Karlsruhe und 303 Gallery, New York Die Ausstellung wird gefördert von der Stanley Thomas Johnson Foundation und der Henry Moore Foundation.

HERAUSGEGEBEN VON CAMDEN ARTS CENTRE 2007 Eingetragene gemeinnützige Organisation 1065829/0, eingetragene Gesellschaft 2947191. **EINGETRAGENER SITZ** Arkwright Road, London, NW3 6DG. Steuernummer 586 9041 03. Alle Rechte vorbehalten. Kein Teil dieser Publikation darf ohne vorherige schriftliche Genehmigung des Herausgebers reproduziert, in einer Datenbank gespeichert oder in irgendeiner Form mit elektronischen oder mechanischen Mitteln übertragen werden, einschließlich Photokopie, Aufnahme und andere Techniken. Der Herausgeber hat sich bemüht, alle Rechteinhaber ausfindig zu machen. Er wird Irrtümer und Auslassungen, die ihm schriftlich mitgeteilt werden, in Folgeauflagen korrigieren.

DANK David Thorpe dankt: Jenni Lomax und Bruce Haines, Camden Arts Centre. Nadia Schneider, Kunsthaus Glarus. Dr. Roland Mönig, Museum Kurhaus Kleve. Catherine Wood, Tate, London. Daniel Baumann, Adolf Wölfli-Stiftung, Kunstmuseum Bern. Maureen Paley, Maureen Paley, London. Thomas Riegger und Jochim Meyer, Meyer Riegger, Karlsruhe. Lisa Spellman, 303 Gallery, New York. Susan Stoops, Worcester Art Museum, Massachusetts. Victoria Adam, Ruth Proctor, Peter Linde Busk, Nick Byrnes, Katherine Gould, Anthea Hamilton, Andrew Palmer, Sara Knowland, James McCann, Joe Walsh, Paul Richards, Hannah Brown, Henna Vainio, Francis Taylor, Emily, Daphne, Dan Davies, Ranko Andjelic, Torbien Anderson, Tomoya Matsuzaki, Nick Sawyer, Norma und Ronald Thorpe. **FÜR** Marie Torbensdatter Hermann.

Camden arts centre · Camden Funded by Camden Council · The Henry Moore Foundation · BRITISH COUNCIL · STANLEY THOMAS JOHNSON FOUNDATION · ARTS COUNCIL ENGLAND